“In 5 Days”

"In 5 Days"

"Grace and Faith On Display"

Zachary Wayne Lavender

XULON PRESS

Xulon Press
2301 Lucien Way #415
Maitland, FL 32751
407.339.4217
www.xulonpress.com

Printed in the United States of America.

ISBN-13: 978-1-63221-740-0
Ebook: 978-1-6322-1741-7

Dedication

It is with overwhelming feelings of gratitude that I dedicate this book to the team and staff of Davita Dialysis and its patients, the transplant team of The University of Chicago-Hyde Park, the team and staff of Scheck & Siress Orthotic, and Prosthetic Care-Oak Park, Ilinois,

Tiffany Collier
Stacy Haywood
Kimberly Hardy
Antoinette Colbert
Antoinette Stewart
Kandyse McCoy-Cunningham
Diedre Robinson
Felicia Joy Daniels
Vanessa McNorton
Albert Tyrone Byrd
Johnnie Lee Patterson
Kimberly Lloyd
Derell Owens
John Angelico
Julie McCay
My family, and

Special Dedication
In loving memory,
Mrs. Charissa Gregory

Table of Contents

Foreword

In 5 Days: Grace and Faith on Display, truly takes you on a personal journey with Zachary through his illness beginning in 2008 until 2019, giving detailed accounts of physical challenges that he had to endure. This book encompasses trials, hope, faith, grace, endurance, and victory. Zachary is transparent in feelings and emotions as he encountered serious health challenges that could have taken his life immediately.

Through his journey, we see God's hand in every diagnosis, amputation, hospital stay, surgery, and dialysis. This book speaks to the trials and challenges that we face in our daily lives and how our God is a mighty Sustainer and Deliverer. Zachary shared his journey and testimony to help others to keep the faith and speak the Word of God, even when you do not see or even feel your breakthrough is near.

God's grace was evident in Zachary's life to sustain him in enduring the physical and emotional pain through his illness. Second Corinthians 12:9 states,

> "But he said to me *'My grace is sufficient for you, for my power is made perfect in weakness, Therefore I will boast all the more gladly about my weaknesses, so that Christ's power may rest in me.'"*

Zachary may have felt weary at times during his journey, but he never lost his faith. He continued to serve the Lord and was active in ministry at his place of worship. In December 2016, he composed a Christmas cantata, *Bethlehem's Joy*, where he facilitated all rehearsals and conducted the choral work with a full orchestra, choir, and children's choir, during the time he was receiving dialysis treatments three times a week.

In 5 Days: Grace and Faith on Display, shows us a glimpse of Zachary's dialysis journey and what happens when you keep your faith in God and don't give up. The victory is yours!

Ms. Felicia Joy Daniels
Diverse Learning Teacher M.A

Acknowledgments

First and foremost, all praises, thanks, honor, and glory belong to God Almighty for His showers of blessings throughout my journey of dialysis treatments. There aren't enough words in the English vocabulary to express enough thanks, gratitude, and overwhelming heart of joy to the entire Davita Dialysis team of nephrologists, nurses, technicians, nurse practitioners, patients, facility administrators, and facility managers for their generous support and encouragement of eight years.

Each of you has made a major impact and contribution to my life in so many valuable ways. From day one of my treatments, you have shown a level of care, consistency, and compassion for those of us who were being challenged and who are still being challenged with end-stage renal disease. The level of work you do and the level of commitment you exemplify goes far and beyond the ***"call of duty."***

Last but not least, I would like to say to each of you, "*Job well done!*" Thank you for all you've done for me while I was under your care. I pray that God's grace, peace, love, and favor will overtake, overwhelm, and overshadow your lives.

Much love,

Zachary Wayne Lavender

Zachary Wayne Lavender
Author

Introduction

> *"Let us, therefore, come boldly to the throne of grace, that we may obtain mercy and find grace to help in time of need."* (Hebrews 4:16-NKJV)

As I was reading this scripture, I found my attitude to be less than that of a Christian. I was displaying a *self-centered and selfish disposition*. How could I be so self-absorbed in not wanting to share my journey in hopes of helping those who are battling with deciding to go through with dialysis? After all, God has extended grace to me in my time of need, and I know all too well the challenges, commitment, and consistency it takes to endure such a traumatic experience of dealing with this rigorous treatment. If God extended grace to me, why can't I share my journey with those men and women who are still in the fight?

"who comforts us in all our tribulation, that we may be able to comfort those who are in any [a]trouble, with the comfort with which we ourselves are comforted by God" (2 Corinthians 1:4).

Imagine being told by your primary physician that your body can no longer eliminate the excess water and waste products. And imagine being told that you must receive dialysis treatments for the rest of your life or until you receive a transplant. Upon hearing this diagnosis, I careened into a depressed and devastating mode. This was a *tough* pill to ingest and digest. At that moment, the enemy was all over my emotions and thoughts. *Am I going to die from this disease*? *Will, I ever have a normal life*? *Will I ever be able to do the things I love to do*? All these thoughts were racing and fighting for my attention.

Every day, there are thousands of people being informed by their physicians they must make a decision regarding dialysis, and there are some cases where the decision must be made immediately. Whatever decision the patient chooses, the path to dialysis can be very daunting, depressing, and disenchanting. I have eight years of experience.

I had come to accept that the dialysis machine is not just another *noisy necessity* but my temporary, dependable, *lifeline*. Many chronic kidney disease patients who prepare to go through the treatments are terrified, traumatized, and timid. This causes the individuals to become detached, demoralized, and disheartened and very concerned about their longevity and quality of life. Dependence on dialysis doesn't constitute a *"death sentence."* Dialysis can sustain your quality of life until you receive your transplant.

Maneuvering the changes that accompany dialysis can be very challenging. It can take several weeks, months, and even years to try and understand the dynamics that go with renal failure and the work of maintaining your sanity. One element to help maintain and manage your sanity is the support of family, friends, the church, your pastor, and those who will keep you in a positive state of mind and atmosphere.

The main purpose of my writing this book is to help those who are going through dialysis treatment while waiting to receive the call, *"We have an offer for you."* Hearing those words can be life-transforming. After being on dialysis for eight years and five months, I'm compelled to encourage, endorse, and exhilarate the lives of so many men, women, children, and families who are daily battling to stay lively, strong, robust, energetic, and, mostly, healthy.

I pray that with every fiber of my being what God has allowed me to pen in these pages will be able to convey the message of hope, help, and healing. I also desire that you gain insight into my journey of strength, struggle, and solace. I pray this book will compel you to strive and stay in a wholesome, healthy, and stress-free environment as you wait on God to do a mighty and miraculous work in your life. This will help you maintain and manage a good healthy dialysis discipline while going through this tough treatment. God wants you to be *fit for the fight, strong for the struggle, and well-suited for the war! "In 5 Days,"* He did it for me, and He can do the same for you.

Zachary Wayne Lavender
Author

CHAPTER ONE

The Broken Glass Experience

"I have said these things to you, that in me you may have peace. In the world, you will have tribulation. But take heart; I have overcome the world." (John 16:33 ESV)

In the summer of 2008, my pastor approached and requested that I organize, plan, and direct the church's summer camp. This was an assignment I had never done before, nor was I familiar with what it would take to start the process. This would be the first time organizing a summer camp. However, I did realize I needed a team that would work with me to bring this project to fruition. Shortly after accepting the assignment, I chose an amazing team. As weeks were swiftly moving, the team worked vigorously in planning and organizing a summer camp that children would never forget. I was absorbed in making certain the assignment was completed and fully executed. For me and the team, this was a top priority. As weeks passed, the team and I began organizing and orchestrating what we considered to be a winning camp for the children. While bringing the camp into reality, something very unusual happened.

On this particular day, I was doing my normal condo cleaning and decided to discard a lot of clutter. On my way to the garbage receptacle, I accidentally stepped on a sharp piece of broken glass. Due to my having diabetes and nephropathy, I had no idea I had stepped on the glass, which was embedded in my right foot. Any substance or object lodged in your foot for some time can cause major problems, a problem I never saw coming. As the day progressed, I would continue to work on building the summer camp. The next day, I was preparing to take a shower so that I could make my appointment to see my primary doctor for my quarterly check-up. As I stepped out of the shower, I noticed a small patch of blood on the bedroom carpet. Of course, I panicked and became agitated and nervous. This was not good. Instead of going to see my primary care physician, I immediately went to John Stroger Hospital Emergency Room. There were people everywhere; however, I knew it was important that I see a doctor to find out why was my foot was bleeding. When it was time to see the doctor, while examining my foot, he discovered a small piece of broken glass that had been lodged under the front part of the foot. My life was about to take a major shift.

During the next weeks, I was directing the summer camp along with the team. I was so engulfed with making certain the camp was well-organized that I forgot about the broken glass situation until I started having very unusual night sweats. I was feeling fatigued and had little-to-no energy. Something was seriously wrong. This had been going on for several days. I didn't say anything to anyone; I just continued with directing the camp. My strength was becoming less, and I was less energized, and I noticed my foot was turning dark and discolored and becoming disfigured. This was not what my foot should look like. At this point, I knew I needed medical attention and quickly. I immediately called my sister and informed her I had been admitted and they wanted to perform surgery to remove part of my foot. The reason I was experiencing fatigue and low energy was that I was in "*septic shock,*" which can become very serious. Because my blood was infected, it was vital that surgery be performed immediately. When my family met with the surgeons, they informed them of what would happen if they did not perform the procedure within twenty-four hours. I would not be writing this book. The procedure was done at 5:00 am, Sunday morning.

What is septic shock/sepsis?

Septic shock is a serious condition that occurs when a body-wide infection leads to dangerously low blood pressure. Septic shock occurs most often in the very old and the very young. It may also occur in people with weakened immune systems. Any type of bacteria can cause septic shock.

After surgery, I was still trying to process what had happened and why this had happened to me. It would take me weeks and months to regain my strength and get back to a somewhat normal life. Because of my limited mobility, the doctors recommended that I not live alone. I needed assistance with day-to-day activities, cooking, walking, and several other things. I discussed with my sister and her husband and informed them of the doctor's recommendations. They did not hesitate to open their doors and invited me to reside with them until I was able to function independently. And for that, I am forever grateful for their generosity and kindness.

In July 2008, I was the guest of my sister and her husband. During my stay with them, I found myself in a very peculiar living environment. I had to make, manage, and maneuver in a new living arrangement. This new living arrangement would transform my perception of myself and how I must embrace change. At the very beginning, I was struggling with living in another person's home. But it wasn't just any home. This was the home of people who loved me and cared about my well-being and health. I was learning to receive from others who had no ill motive or ill intent. Eventually, the stay was very pleasant and enjoyable. Along with my family, we made it work!

The next several months were very challenging. I had to learn to shower, cook, clean, and do other activities with one foot. That's when the crutches became my *BFF* (*best friend forever*). I would soon master the art of maneuvering with these metal poles. I had no other choice. It was either learn how to use them to my advantage or be confined to a wheelchair. I refused to be manipulated and confined by any device or object. I was determined to work at making the crutches work in my favor. I didn't have the crutches much longer. I decided to be fitted for a prosthetic device. This would allow me more range of motion, mobility, freedom, and the opportunity to become more independent. Later in the year, I was fitted with the prosthetic, and it proved to be an overwhelming success.

Several months had passed, and it was time for me to visit my primary doctor for my post-surgery evaluation. Before my visit, I noticed when I would urinate, there was an odor, and my urine was slightly dark, cloudy, and foamy. This was not normal, and I knew something was wrong. When I made my visit to see my primary, I informed him of my urine issue. Of course, he had blood work done to determine what was brewing. The next day after my visit, my primary called and informed me that my "creatinine levels" were not normal and they were slightly elevated, which meant that my kidneys were not functioning at 100 percent. At this point, I was on the radar for renal failure disease. The doctor had me schedule an appointment every three months to determine my creatinine levels, and on each visit, the levels were not where they should be. There were several main causes of my renal failure:

- Diabetes
- High Blood Pressure
- Poor Diet

My nephrologist made a medical decision that would change my life. He decided it was time to prepare me for hemodialysis. Later that year (October 2010), I would have the surgery to implant an AV fistula under the skin of my left arm.

What is an AV fistula?

A surgeon connects an artery to a vein, usually in your arm, to create an AV fistula. An artery is a blood vessel that carries blood away from your heart. The AV fistula is a blood vessel made wider and stronger by a surgeon to handle the needles that allow blood to flow out to and return from a dialysis terminal.

After the fistula was implanted, the thought of having dialysis was always on my mind. I had so many questions for God. So much I didn't understand regarding my situation and so much of dialysis drama wasn't making any sense.

There were times I wanted to cry, but I couldn't. There were times I wanted to *hate* God, but I couldn't. I had to pull myself together. After I composed my thoughts and composure, Romans 8:28 reminded me of this,

> *"And we know that in **ALL** things God works for the good of those who love Him, who have been called according to **His** purpose."*

Shortly after reading this, things became a lot clearer. God was going to use the amputation and dialysis for His purpose and my good!

Moving forward with the thoughts of having to go through with dialysis would eventually put me in a state of depression. I knew absolutely nothing about dialysis. I knew nothing about the long-term effects it would have on my mind, body and spirit. I was walking into unknown and unfamiliar territory. So, I decided to do my research and study on the subject. After my discovery and analysis, I was more at peace. I had a greater understanding and knowledge of this new phase that would soon invade my life. Maneuvering the changes that accompany dialysis was very scary and sometimes unknowing. Not only did I have to make adjustments, but my family was also greatly affected as well.

Several weeks after the procedure, I wasn't feeling my best. I called to make an appointment to see my primary care doctor. He did bloodwork, ran test, and the labs showed my creatinine levels had spiked drastically. She informed me to go immediately to the University of Chicago Emergency Room. On Thursday, June 16, 2011, I would have my first dialysis treatment. I was terrified! The technician assured me I would do well and not to worry, that he would take good care of me. This was the longest four hours ever. I thought the treatment would never end. I'm still fascinated that a machine can clean your blood, eliminate the excess water, discard the toxins, and then return the blood. While all of this is transpiring, the machine's chemicals never come in contact with your blood. *This is mind-blowing!* At the end of the treatment, I was exhausted and had an extreme appetite, which meant that the treatment was a success. Praise the Lord!

Over the weekend, I had plenty of time to prepare for my next treatment, which began Monday at 5:30 am. I was assigned to Davita Dialysis, located at 51st & Lake Park in Chicago. The blessing in being assigned to this facility is that I lived one block away. I was within walking distance (*around the corner*). My first day at this facility is one I will never forget. On the morning of my treatment, I received a call from the charge nurse reminding me of my treatment and to make sure I did not forget. I made my dialysis debut at 5:15 am to check out the facility and ask a ton of questions. The staff were pleasant and made certain I was comfortable and relaxed during treatment. Once I was settled and the treatment began, it would take me no time to get acquainted with the technicians and dialysis format. Of course, it would take time for me to get accustomed to getting up at the break of dawn. I knew that getting up, getting dressed, and going in was an overwhelming commitment; however, I wasn't going to allow my temporary meltdowns to interfere with what God was doing in my life. When I became overwhelmed and depressed, I would constantly think back to Romans 8:28,

> *"And we know that in* ***ALL*** *things God works for the good of those who love Him, who have been called according to* ***His*** *purpose."*

This scripture pulled me through the entire duration of my having treatments. The first two years of dialysis were brutal, to the point of my wanting to give up and not go through with the treatment. Of course, when I came to my senses, *it was just a fleeting thought*. I could not and would not give the enemy the advantage. I couldn't surrender to his taunting tactics. I was determined to rely totally on God for strength and sustenance. I remembered and reflected on Isaiah 41:10 (NKJV),

> *"So do not fear, for I am with you; do not be dismayed, for I am your God. I will strengthen you and help you*; I *will uphold you with my righteous right hand."*

CHAPTER TWO

The Challenge

"For I, the Lord your God, hold your right hand; It is I who say to you, 'Fear not, I am the one who helps you.'" (Isaiah 41:13-ESV)

Dialysis was first introduced in the 1940s. Its main objective was intended to be a lifesaving treatment designed to allow the patient an opportunity to experience life without too many limitations. Concentrating on young patients with acute renal failure, it helped them until their kidneys were strong enough to function without the treatment. In this twenty-first century, dialysis has been transformed. It is currently used as a maintenance treatment as frequently as for acute issues. However, a shift has occurred in the treatment and frequency with which it's offered to different patient populations.

Before I could begin my first treatment at Davita Dialysis (Monday, June 20, 2011), my family and I were scheduled to meet with the facility manager. This was an informational meeting to give us insight into the world of dialysis. He was very thorough and efficient. My family had a lot of questions regarding the treatment and the short-term and long-term effects it would have on my quality of life. He informed me of my options for treatment, including available treatments and transplantation. In addition to the well-organized presentation, the facility manager informed me of my being the expert regarding my commitment, consistency, values, and goals and the nephrologist being the expert in the prognosis and treatment options, both of which need to be considered as a part of the process.

The first two years were a struggle regarding my body and how it was responding to the treatment. I realized the key to successful treatment was consistency in making sure I was following protocol and being compliant with the rules, regulations, and standards of Davita's commitment to professional care. For you to understand what I had to go through for eight years and five months, I must explain the dynamics of hemodialysis.

What is hemodialysis?

While healthy kidneys have several functions in the body, the most well-known job is to produce urine. When kidney function goes below 10 to 15 percent, kidneys are no longer able to filter the blood and make urine. This causes toxins to build up in the body, along with excess fluid.

As you have just read, I hope you have a greater understanding of the highs and lows of what I experienced for eight years and five months (1,212 treatments). During my time of being on dialysis, all treatments were at the same facility. I grew accustomed to the family atmosphere at Lake Park and Kenwood Dialysis and what they afforded me. The most memorable moment of being in this facility is that I was able to minister to several patients. I saw their pain, their hurt, their depression, their anxiety, their restlessness, their anger, their weary spirits, and those who wanted to throw in the towel and give up on life. I realized this was the perfect opportunity for me to show the love of Christ. I was quickly reminded of the Word of God in Ephesians 3:13 (NKJV),

"Therefore I ask that you do not lose heart at my tribulations for you, which is your glory."

To *"lose heart"* is to become attached to discouragement, disappointment, and defeat. We will always *lose heart* and feel defeated when there's no connection *to God* and no relationship *with God*. We connect with Him through ***prayer***. When I started dialysis, my prayer life was weak, ineffective, and not recognized by God. The reason I say it was weak, ineffective, and not recognized by God is that I had no connection to Him. How could I make an impact in the lives of those who I ministered to when there was no connection to God? As it says in John 15:4 (MSG),

> *"Live in me. Make your home in me just as I do in you. In the same way that a branch can't bear grapes by itself but only by being joined to the vine, you can't bear fruit unless you are joined with me."*

This was a wake-up call for me. I had work to do. Every patient that God allowed me to minister to needed the same thing. We needed *"earthly permission for heavenly interference*!" We needed to bombard the throne of heaven to help us not to "*lose heart*." I was taking a huge risk when I decided to have conversations with some of the patients about the power of prayer and the many benefits of establishing a relationship with Christ. I needed to obey what God had given me to do. Every conversation I had with some of the patients, *God moved profoundly*!

For an entire year, God allowed me to write letters of encouragement, scriptures, and quotes and pass them on to the patients. Some were receptive, and some were not. However, my focus was concentrating on those who wanted to be uplifted and inspired to keep fighting. I clearly remember having a conversation with one patient (*who shall remain anonymous*), and his exact words were, *"Mr. Lavender, I'm so tired, and I don't want to do this anymore. I don't feel like this is helping me. When the weather turns cold, I'm not coming anymore."* After the conversation, I always wondered why he chose to share this with me. We had had conversations before but never to this degree. Then I thought, *He must've seen something in me that made him trust me enough to share this with me.* That same evening, I drafted a two-page letter of encouragement. To this day, he's still holding on, and he has not given up the fight! Praise the Lord!

Shortly after starting dialysis, I wasn't sure when I should begin the process of getting on the kidney transplant list. As I begin research on the topic, I discovered it's best to explore transplant early in your diagnosis before you need to start dialysis (*I knew nothing of this before starting treatment*). This way, you might be able to get a transplant without ever needing to start dialysis. I had a conversation with my nephrologist and primary physician, and they highly recommended that I pursue the possibility of receiving a kidney transplant. Before I could be considered a candidate for the transplant, I would have to undergo a plethora of tests.

- Blood and tissue type
- Test for HIV

- Prostate exam (for men)/Mammogram (for women)
- Heart and lung exams
- Kidney and liver test
- Colon exam (colonoscopy)
- Chest X-ray
- CT (computed tomography) of your abdomen (to see the blood vessels and structure of your kidneys)

After taking the kidney transplant evaluation, I met with the transplant team at the University of Chicago, and they indicated that I was a good candidate for the transplant. As of September 2011, I was officially on the transplant list. This was exciting. At this stage, I needed to comply with all transplant guidelines and protocols so that I would remain active on the list. There were certain criteria I had to follow.

Because I had been diagnosed with end-stage renal disease (*ESRD*) in 2010, this qualified me as the perfect candidate. There were certain areas I was responsible for complying with. Once I discovered I was a good candidate to receive a transplant, preparing for surgery could start immediately, even though I might need to wait for a donor organ (in my case, eight years and five months). There are some things you can do before the transplant to ensure you're well-prepared, to include:

- Attend all the appointments and education as directed by your transplant care team.

- Take all your medications prescribed by your primary physician.
- If you smoke, you should *quit immediately* ***(smoking can retard your healing process.)***
- Eat healthy, foods such as fruit, vegetables, whole grains, and lean proteins.
- Exercise to maintain and manage your energy level as you are able.
- Get plenty of rest.
- Make certain your caregiver arrangements are in place. If your caregiver should need to step away during your waiting period, identify someone who's able to step in (*family, friends, coworkers, neighbors, church family, etc.*).

Emotional Preparedness

Preparing yourself emotionally for your transplant surgery is just as important as being medically and practically prepared. You might experience feelings of frustration or anxiety over waiting for an organ to become available. Exposing yourself to dialysis can result in contracting infections.

At this stage, I'd been on dialysis for four years, and it had been a journey. It was the summer of 2012, and I was experiencing some discomfort in my right shoulder. This persisted for several weeks, after which I made an appointment to see my primary physician. There were all sorts of blood work and labs done, and her medical diagnosis was *"muscle spasms."* Of course, I didn't question her diagnosis. However, I knew it was much more than muscle spasms because the pain lingered for months. It would go away and later return. When the pain returned, it was a lot worse than before.

Later in the year, I was having a very difficult time moving my shoulder, sleeping, and sitting for an extended amount of time. I was dealing with the shoulder issue while consistently going to dialysis. In January 2013, while being dialyzed, I started experiencing a severe case of diarrhea. The technicians were aggressively working to take me off the machine, and I was able to make it to the restroom. As I was trying to get off the commode, I wasn't able to move my upper body. It was as if I had been paralyzed. At this stage, it had become very serious. The charge nurse called 9-1-1, and I was rushed to The University of Chicago (Hyde Park). Upon my arrival at the hospital, I was admitted immediately. I was given a load of fluids so that my vitals would stabilize. The doctors ran all sorts of tests and discovered there was an abscess near my spine and that was the culprit causing the right shoulder pain. I had contracted an infection called *"osteomyelitis."*

What is osteomyelitis?

Osteomyelitis is a bone infection. The infection can reach the bone by traveling through the bloodstream or spreading from nearby tissue. Infections can also begin in the bone itself if an injury exposes the bone to germs.

So the question on the table was, *"How did I contract this bone infection?"* The only explanation was dialysis. Earlier in the year, I had been approached by the staff to inform me that I was a candidate for a buttonhole. I must explain this procedure and how it led to my contracting osteomyelitis.

What is a buttonhole technique?

The buttonhole technique is a way to "cannulate," which means "to insert dialysis needles." Instead of sharp, pointed needles, dull needles are placed into the same holes on your fistula every time you have dialysis.

Who can use the buttonhole technique?

The buttonhole technique can only be used by patients with an AV fistula and cannot be used by those with an AV graft. It can be used by patients who self-cannulate (insert their needles) either at home or in a dialysis center after approval from their healthcare provider.

It is important to make sure you perform the buttonhole technique in the right way to reduce problems.

Infection is the biggest concern with this technique. But knowing how to care for your buttonhole sites will keep them problem-free for a very long time. Here are some ways to reduce your risks:

Clean skin and buttonhole sites very well

Because buttonhole sites are permanent exit sites, bacteria (germs) will collect around them. Staph (short for *Staphylococcus*) is a type of bacteria commonly found on the skin that is generally harmless but can cause infection if sterile technique is not used when caring for your access. Also, patients on dialysis have more staph germs on their skin than the general population. Therefore, extra cleaning is needed, and the following are steps to take:

- Wash the access before sitting down to be dialyzed/cannulate.
- Before removing scabs, thoroughly disinfect the site.
- Remove scabs completely.
- Disinfect one more time.
- Let skin dry.
- Cannulate/dialyze.

The reason for my contracting osteomyelitis is that the technician did not remove and thoroughly clean the scab surrounding the access. When the needle is inserted and the scab has not been thoroughly removed, you're at high risk for bacteria to enter the body, causing germs to make contact with the blood, which exposes the patient to *a serious bone infection*.

The next step for me dealing with this bone infection was surgery to eradicate the infected area. When the doctors did the ultrasound, they noticed an abscess had formed near my spine. *This was a very serious surgical procedure*. The first surgery was performed, yet I was still in much pain. More tests were done, and the doctors discovered that some of the infected areas had not been removed. Once again, I was back in the OR (operating room) for another surgery. In addition to having two surgeries within a week, I contracted pneumonia in both lungs. My overall stay in the hospital was a total of two weeks.

It was time for me to leave the hospital and head to rehab at Schwab Rehabilitation Center. When I was admitted, I wasn't doing well. I wasn't able to walk or stand, and I had very little mobility. With the amazing help of the physical therapist, occupational therapist, and entire staff, I was able to leave in two weeks. The therapy was scheduled for four weeks to completely recover. However, I was not going to be there that length of time. I knew the moment I was wheeled in rehab that I had work to do. Every morning at 6:00 am, I was wide awake, bathed, and fully dressed. My adrenaline and determination would not allow this setback to stop me from doing what I needed to do—walk, stand, and regain my mobility. After two weeks of very aggressive and intense therapy, I was able to leave.

CHAPTER THREE

The Chamber

Therefore I say to you, do not worry about your life, what you will eat or what you will drink; nor about your body, what you will put on. Is not life more than food and the body more than clothing? Look at the birds of the air, for they neither sow nor reap nor gather into barns; yet your heavenly Father feeds them. Are you not of more value than they? Which of you by worrying can add one cubit to his stature? "So why do you worry about clothing? Consider the lilies of the field, how they grow: they neither toil nor spin; and yet I say to you that even Solomon in all his glory was not arrayed like one of these.

> *Now if God so clothes the grass of the field, which today is, and tomorrow is thrown into the oven, will He not much more clothe you, O you of little faith? "Therefore do not worry, saying, 'What shall we eat?' or 'What shall we drink?' or 'What shall we wear?' For after all these things the Gentiles seek. For your heavenly Father knows that you need all these things. But seek first the kingdom of God and His righteousness, and all these things shall be added to you. Therefore do not worry about tomorrow, for tomorrow will worry about its own things. Sufficient for the day is its own trouble.* (Matthew 6:25-34 NKJV)

So far I've shared with you how God was teaching me how to handle the broken-glass experience. I never thought I would go through something so dramatic, devastating, and debilitating. Accepting I had to decide to part with my foot was overwhelming. It left me with a lot of anxiety and uncertainties. I never thought I would be wearing a prosthetic. I never imagined not having a part of the body I've had my entire life. One thing this ordeal has taught me: *"Don't take anything for granted. It can be with you one moment, and the next, it's gone."* This was just the beginning of a situation that would take me into a whirlwind of emotions. When I speak of a whirlwind, that's exactly what it was—a whirlwind that was designed to deliver stress, stress, and more stress. Even in this stressful situation, though, God had another plan.

In July 2008, the doctors delivered the news that would change the trajectory of my life. The news that I must have surgery to amputate my right foot resulted in a drastically different outlook for my future (*so I thought*) than the one I had previously envisioned. Some great things I felt certain would be accomplished were suddenly interrupted and out of my grasp (*so I thought*). At that moment, I was tempted to become discouraged, disengaged, and disenchanted about my future. I couldn't imagine not being able to fulfill the purpose God had called, appointed, and custom-designed for me to fulfill. I couldn't imagine not being able to work with children. I couldn't imagine not being able to write, score, and compose music. All these things drowned my thoughts. So that I could get through this very challenging ordeal, I had to put everything in its proper perspective and context. I was quickly reminded of Philippians 4:8 (MSG):

> *Summing it all up, friends, I'd say you'll do best by filling your minds and meditating on things true, noble, reputable, authentic, compelling, gracious—the best, not the worst; the beautiful, not the ugly; things to praise, not things to curse. Put into practice what you learned from me, what you heard and saw and realized. Do that, and God, who makes*

> *everything work together, will work you into his most excellent harmonies.*

Like many Christians in challenging times, I found myself searching for scriptures that would help me understand the ***"what"*** and the ***"why."*** Again, I was reminded of Jeremiah 29:10-11 (MSG),

> *"This is God's Word on the subject: 'As soon as Babylon's seventy years are up and not a day before, I'll show up and take care of you as I promised and bring you back home. I know what I'm doing. I have it all planned out—plans to take care of you, not abandon you, plans to give you the future you hope for.'"*

It's refreshing and reassuring amid trouble that God has a plan for me and it's a plan that far outweighs anything I could ever face. The Word of God confirms this,

> *"God is our refuge and strength; a very present help in the time of trouble...Be still and know that I am God. I will be exalted among the nations; I will be exalted in the earth"* (Ps. 46:1, 10 NKJV).

Moreover, there's a danger in leaning on *our* understanding and holding on to *our* idea of what the Lord's plans for our lives, welfare, future, and hope. Rather, we should let the *whole* Word of God dictate His plans, His will, and His agenda to rule and reign in our lives and over our lives. I had come to the reality of God's Word as the focus of understanding my situation. (Proverbs 3:5-6 MSG) says this:

> *"Trust God from the bottom of your heart; don't try to figure out everything on your own. Listen for God's voice in everything you do, everywhere you go. He's the one who will keep you on track."*

At this juncture, I'd been wearing my prosthetic since 2008 (six years). I had no issues or concerns, other than the usual maintenance, occasional fitting, and refitting. The prosthetist team at Scheck & Siress (Oak Park, Illinois) made certain my device was in mint condition. I never worried about making appointments or reaching out to the team when I needed impromptu visits. Even when my weight would fluctuate, I could always depend on the team to make a professional decision. At some point, my stump (amputation) was beginning to breakdown. Sores and ulcers were developing on the stump. I knew something had to be done to alleviate this problem. I was concerned because the healing wasn't looking very promising.

Later in the year, I was having a conversation with a patient at dialysis, and she highly recommended that I see her wound care doctor at Weiss Memorial Hospital.

Of course, I called and made an appointment. Upon my arrival, I had a consultation with the doctor to share with her my medical history and the wound developing on my foot. Upon examining my foot, blood work, and X-rays, it was determined I once again had contracted osteomyelitis due to the breakdown and ulcer. But this time, the infection had invaded the bone in my foot. She went on to explain the treatment and the necessity of the treatments I would receive while under her care. The treatment was called *"hyperbaric oxygen therapy."* You're probably wondering, *what is hyperbaric oxygen therapy?*

Hyperbaric oxygen therapy is a specialized treatment intended to speed the healing process. Hyperbaric oxygen therapy, or HBO, is an innovative treatment that allows rapid healing far beyond what would happen naturally. Wounds require oxygen to heal and thus will heal more quickly in a pressurized 100 percent oxygen environment (New York Center for Plastic & Laser Surgery).

I began HBO in February 2014 and concluded in May 2014. I received sixty treatments within three months, which meant I had to sit inside this contraption *(the chamber)* for *two hours five days a week*. What baffled me is that I would go home, cook an entire meal, clean the apartment, and occasionally sit at the piano and compose a piece of music. I wondered, "*where did all this energy come from?*" "*How am I able to do all these activities after my body has been ravaged with all sorts of fluids and medications*?" There were times I didn't understand how my body endured all the treatments of dialysis and hyperbaric oxygen therapy. A majority of the time after leaving therapy, though, I would have a huge surge of energy.

I asked myself these questions: *"Where can I go to find strength when I feel weak? Where can I go to find an understanding of my circumstance?"* The answer was staring me in the face. The Bible has been given to all men to find comfort, relief, peace, understanding, and strength for difficult times and encouragement of our faith when we feel weak, worn, and weary. Satan's objective is to make us feel weak, useless, and ultimately defeated. We must fight his attacks, tricks, and tactics against our spirit, mind, body, and soul with the truth of Scripture. This is what the Word of God says about strength:

- *"**My** grace is enough; it's all you need. **My** strength comes into its own in your weakness." (2 Corinthians 12:9)*
- *"Fear not, for **I** am with you; be not dismayed, for **I** am your God; **I** will strengthen you, **I** will help you, **I** will uphold you with **My** righteous right hand." (Isaiah 41:10)*
- *"Be strong and courageous. Do not fear or be in dread of them, for it is the LORD your God who goes with you. **He** will not leave you or forsake you." (Deuteronomy 31:6)*
- *"I can do all things through **Him** who strengthens me." (Philippians 4:13)*

The reason I was able to develop the strength, energy, resilience, and fight was simple. It was God all the time. He was my sustainer, my source, and my strength. He was my rock, my refuge, and my rest. There's no way I could have endured six years of dialysis and three months of HBO therapy without the strength of my Heavenly Father. There's no way I would have been able to continue working in the ministry while having treatments without God's hand on me. It was God's strength that carried me.

While continuing HBO treatments, it seemed as if the therapy wasn't doing what the doctors had anticipated. The infection became more aggressive. This is where I needed to make another major health decision. This time the decision I had to make would again cause me to think about my health and the reason I was going through this again. I was becoming more and more apprehensive about having to amputate the lower portion of my right leg *(below the knee/ BKA)*. Yes, this was the decision I had to make. Just a few years earlier, I had been dealing with having to amputate my toes on my right foot. Now, this! *"How much more could I handle? How much more would God allow me to go through? How much more could I deal with regarding my health?"* This was just too much. I had to let the truth of God's Word—not the amputation, not my situation, not my flesh, and certainly, not my understanding—define my decision. The truth is that God never promises not to put more on us than we can handle. However, He does promise us that He will be there to guide us through whatever circumstances we're faced with. Let's take a closer look at 1 Corinthians 10:13 (NKJV)

> *"No temptation has overtaken you except such as is common to man; but God is faithful, who will not allow you to be tempted beyond what you are able, but with the temptation will also make a way of escape, that you may be able to bear it."*

If you've been a Christian for some time, then I'm sure you've heard someone say, *"God won't give you more than you can handle."* I've heard pastors, biblical scholars, theologians, and many Christians make this erroneous statement. However, we need to rethink critically about this statement based on what the Bible says. *Are we rightly dividing the Word of Truth? Are we interpreting Scripture in its proper context?*

Please allow me to make a case that this statement is false and can be found nowhere in Scripture. A majority of godly, mature, and more knowledgeable Christians may disagree with me. However, we can have a healthy conversation regarding the correct interpretation of this passage of Scripture. My objective is not to make anyone feel inferior, condemned, or even attacked but rather to help us sharpen our understanding of Scripture so we can be more precise, practical, positive, and helpful as we minister to others who may be struggling and suffering.

Why do I believe the statement, *"God won't give you more than you can handle,"* is futile and fruitless? Here are two reasons:

(1) *The Word of God does not support or teach this.*
(2) The Bible teaches the opposite truth *(at times, God does give us more than we can handle)*. Also, I think we can give more accurate and authentic encouragement to those who are struggling and suffering.

Many Christians believe that 1 Corinthians 10:13 teaches, *"God won't give you more than you can handle."* However, this verse states,

> *"No temptation has overtaken you that is not common to man. God is faithful, and He will not let you be tempted beyond your ability, but with the temptation, He will provide the way of escape, that you may be able to endure it."*

Many ministries and Christians who teach that "*God won't give you more than you can handle"* explain that the word *"temptation,"* can refer to a temptation to sin, a trial, or any type of suffering. They are correct. The Greek word used here for *"temptation"* can be used to speak of both suffering and sin. If you look in a Greek lexicon, it will show *"testing" or "trial"* as possible ways this word can be translated. Why, then, is it wrong to claim that this verse is addressing testing, trials, and suffering? God, through Paul, is telling us in this passage that *no one will be tempted to* ***"sin"*** beyond what he or she can bear. That is astoundingly good news! Praise God for His grace to us. However, this passage does not teach that a person will not face a trial or suffering beyond what he/she can bear. Let's take a closer look at 2 Corinthians 1:8-11:

> *For we do not want you to be ignorant, brethren, of our trouble which came to us in Asia: that we were burdened beyond measure, above strength, so that we despaired even of life. Yes, we had the sentence of death in ourselves, that we should not trust in ourselves but in God who raises the dead, who delivered us from so great a death, and does deliver us; in whom we trust that He will still deliver us, you also helping together in prayer for us, that thanks may be given by many persons on our behalf for the gift granted to us through many.*

Paul's narrative clearly shows that God may give us more suffering than we can handle.

Paul says that he and his companions were, *"so utterly burdened beyond our strength that we despaired of life itself (**they wanted to die**)."* He continues by saying, *"Indeed, we* *felt that we had received the sentence of death.* ***But that was to make us rely not on ourselves but on God who raises the dead.*** *He delivered us from such a deadly peril, and He will deliver us. On Him, we have set our hope that He will deliver us again."*

These scriptures show us that Paul was burdened beyond his strength and ability. To be burdened beyond one's strength is to be given more than he or she can handle. God, through Paul, is saying that *"anyone"* can experience more suffering than he or she can handle. I suggest that we cease saying, *"God won't give you more than you can handle,"* and begin speaking and encouraging people by saying, *"God will give you all the grace you need in every situation you face."*

After I took the time to study this scripture, I understood why I was going through this and who would bring me through it and out of it. *At times, God will give me more than I can handle.* I had to reflect on what He had already done for me. If He brought me through the first surgery, He would bring me through the others.

I eventually had a conversation with my wound care doctor, and she assured me that the amputation would improve my quality of life and allow me the liberty of movement and mobility. Shortly after the conversation, we started the process of preparing for the procedure. On Monday, January 12, 2015, the procedure was performed to amputate my right leg below the knee. I was at peace with everything. God again showed me that it was Him all the time. He showed me that He was in charge. He showed me that all power belongs to Him and that *"He will give me all the grace I need in every situation I face."*

CHAPTER FOUR

God's Time-Table!

"And let us not grow weary of doing good, for in due season we will reap, if we do not give up." (Ecclesiastes 6:9-ESV)

Zachary Wayne Lavender—fifty-eight years of age, a musician, composer, author, Christian, and agent of change. Mr. Lavender is CEO of the Sanctuary of Refuge and Set Apart Fresh Start. Both organizations and support ministries are visions designed to help men and women who struggle with the practice of homosexuality and families who may be affected understand the dynamics of homosexuality and what it takes to leave the practice and live according to God's Word. Raised and born in Monroe, Louisiana, he is dedicated and committed to his calling, assignment, and created purpose. Zachary is an *extrovert* who loves all people and tries to be an inspiration and encouragement to see God's people living and pursuing the life God predestined for them.

That's why when I learned in 2009 that I had *end-stage renal disease (ESRD)*, a disease that eventually leads to dialysis, there was no time for menial or insignificant side-bar conversations. There was work to be done!

Kidney disease (ESRD) can be progressive. The length of each stage varies and depends on how your kidney disease is treated, especially concerning your diet and whether your doctor recommends dialysis. Chronic kidney disease typically doesn't reach the end stage until ten to twenty years after you're diagnosed. ESRD is the fifth and final stage of the progression of chronic kidney disease before starting dialysis.

In 2008, shortly after my first amputation, I was experiencing excessive urinating, lethargy, and dry mouth and was consuming a large number of fluids. This was very unusual and something I had never experienced. This is when my nephrologist diagnosed me with ESRD/end-stage renal disease. Over fourteen months, my kidney function slowly declined to the degree that my doctor was concerned about the possibility I might need to prepare for dialysis. In May 2010, my kidney function took another hit and dropped below 10 percent, which meant I would soon start dialysis. This was *a hard pill to swallow.* However, it had to happen.

Finally, in October 2010, I had surgery to implant a fistula. The surgery was performed at John Stroger Hospital.

The reason I'm revisiting my dialysis and AV fistula is to make certain you have a greater understanding of what led to dialysis. Prepare to have your mind *blown*! Before I get to the grandeur of the story, I must walk you through the *five days* before receiving the *kidney transplant.*

Like all people who are waiting for transplantation, I didn't have the option of a transplant from a living donor. I asked my siblings, and they declined. I believe their reasons for declining were fear and having their own health issues. In my case, either option, living or deceased, could present a major challenge when it came to finding a blood and tissue match. My hindrance was that I had *high antibodies*, which meant I would have a longer waiting period (*five to eight years*). Whoever the donor, he or she too must have high antibodies, or I could run the risk of my body rejecting the kidney. You're probably wondering, *what are high antibodies*?

What are high antibodies?

Our immune system naturally forms antibodies as a protective response against bacteria and viruses. In the context of transplantation, antibodies are good when they are ready to attack foreign invaders that can lead to illness, but antibodies can also be ready to attack foreign tissue, such as a new kidney transplant.

How did I contract high antibodies?

Antibodies are formed by the immune system when you are exposed to proteins that appear similar to tissue types. This most commonly occurs in the setting of previous transplantation, pregnancy, or *blood transfusion*.

I needed to be offered a kidney transplant within the next few years. It was always weighing heavy on my mind, yet I was very ambitious about the certainty of being offered an organ. On Thursday, March 1, 2018, at 4:30 am, I turned off my cell phone, not thinking I might get a call with an offer. I was awakened by my land-line phone. Something spoke to me and said, *"That's an offer."* So, I immediately turned on my cell. As quickly as I turned on the phone, it rang. It was my transplant coordinator with a kidney offer. She informed me that a donor had been found and that they were offering me the kidney if the other patient declined the offer. Several hours later, she called and informed me that the other person had accepted the offer. I must be honest. I was disappointed and a bit distraught. I had thought this was the one. After all, I had been on the waiting list for six years and nine months. I was under the impression that my time had come. My transplant coordinator kept insisting that I continue to *wait*, but my hopes of receiving a kidney weren't looking favorable.

The Weight in Waiting

In the twenty-first century, so that we remain relevant and ready, we must come to understand that technology doesn't always function at its highest level. In other words, it will break down and malfunction. When this happens, we proceed to dial tech support and carefully listen to instructions given by a recording. We press one button after another, trying to reach some sort of help with our situation. At some point, the phone rings and rings, and we are relieved when we finally hear a voice on the other end of the call. It's usually someone from another country or someone you're having a difficult time understanding, though. The purpose of calling was to get a resolution regarding my technical issue. Just when I thought I was about to have my issue resolved, I got another recording, *"Please wait for the next available agent. Your* ***wait*** *time is two minutes."* My wait time was eight years and five months!

Most of us don't like waiting and being put on hold. Let's be honest—it can be annoying! This can take us out of character (at least myself) and bring out the worst in us. Our Creator knows every one of us, down to the hairs on our head, and He knows what makes us tick, our weaknesses and our shortcomings. Waiting is not something we take lightly. Waiting is not something that we're born with. Waiting is not something you take off and put on. It's a lifelong process.

During the time of waiting to receive my kidney transplant, I discovered that waiting wasn't a waste of time. However, it was the perfect opportunity to develop, grow and mature in character, faith, and wisdom. Whenever the weight *(heaviness)* and the wait *(attitude)* feel impossible, do all you can to focus on developing and building patience, perseverance, and your relationship with Jesus Christ. This is not the time to fret or frown. Spend time in the Word of God, and you will discover that God's strength (*His weight, His glory)* is perfect, and He will provide you the ability to endure when you willingly submit to His authority and will. Remember, the *wait* can be *weighty,* but wait on the Lord.

> *"But those who wait on the Lord shall renew their strength; They shall mount up with wings like eagles, They shall run and not be weary, They shall walk and not faint."* (Isaiah 40:31 NKJV)

After the offer and a crushed spirit, I resumed my regularly scheduled dialysis treatments. Of course, I wanted the offer to be successful, yet I had to deal with the fact it might not happen on my schedule. However, it was all in God's time and His hands. At this juncture, I'd been on dialysis six years and nine months, and I was struggling with understanding God's timetable. *How could I know what God's timing looked like*? First and foremost, I needed to understand that God's timetable is perfect, unblemished, flawless and absolute. Just as all of God's ways are perfect, His timing is never early, and it's never too late. It's always on time in perfect order.

> *"What a God! His road stretches straight and smooth.* ***Every God-direction is road-tested.*** *Everyone who runs toward him makes it."* (Psalm 18:30 MSG)

> *"But when the* ***right time*** *came, God sent his Son, born of a woman, subject to the law."* (Galatians 4:4 NLT)

No event in history has ever put a damper, delay, or deterrent on the timing of God's eternal plan or purpose. I thought by understanding God's timing, it would make my waiting for a kidney a little easier. That's not always the case. Humanly, we can make waiting for God's impeccable timing a challenging task. The microwave mentality and not wanting to wait, often find it difficult to wait for anything or anyone. We want what we want now, this very moment, not caring who we inconvenience and clearly not understanding the consequences of waiting and developing the fruit of ***patience***. Look at what Galatians 5:22 (NLT) says,

> *"But the Holy Spirit produces this kind of fruit in our lives: love, joy, peace,* ***patience,*** *kindness, goodness, faithfulness."*

The Word of God makes it very clear that God is pleased with us when we develop and demonstrate the fruit of the Spirit,

> *"Be still in the presence of the Lord, and **wait** patiently for him to act."* (Psalm 37:7 NLT)

> *"The Lord is good to those who **wait** for him."* (Lamentations 3:25 NKJV)

Another crucial element to understanding God's timing is *complete and total trust*. Our ability to wait on God is attributed to how much we put our trust in Him. When we trust in God with all our mind, body, soul, and strength and not lean on our intellect and understanding, abandoning dependence on ourselves, He will graciously lead us in the right direction.

> *"Trust in the Lord with all your heart, And lean not on your own understanding; In all your ways acknowledge Him, And He shall direct your paths."* (Proverbs 3:5-6 NKJV)

To truly trust God, we must know Him. You cannot trust in someone or something you have no relationship with. What and who we trust, we're familiar and comfortable with being around and in proximity to. Often, God will use situations, challenges, trials, tribulations, and death to strengthen our patience, giving our Christian walk fervor and fight to mature and become complete. James 1:3-4 (NKJV) says,

> *"Knowing that the testing of your faith produces* ***patience.*** *But let* ***patience*** *have its perfect work, that you may be* ***perfect*** *and complete, lacking nothing."*

I was at a crossroads and close to receiving the call that would transform my life. What was required of me was *patience* and *reliance* on God's timetable to manifest. It wasn't my place to tell God what to do, how to do it, or when to do it. He's sovereign, and He can do what He chooses to do. He can choose how He wants to do it, and He can choose who He wants to do it through. He doesn't need my permission, and He doesn't need my input. He's God all by Himself!

'DAY ONE'

It was Saturday morning, December 14, 2019. One of my top priorities is spending time meditating on the Word of God. This particular morning was unusual in the sense of my wanting to study with Dr. Tony Evans and his teachings on prayer. During this study session, he was teaching from the book of Luke 17:37, 18:1-8, and he entitled the message, *"Power in Prayer."*

"And they said to him, 'Where, Lord?' He said to them, 'Where the corpse is, there the vultures will gather.'" (Luke 17:37 ESV)

And he told them a parable to the effect that they ought always to pray and not lose heart. He said, "In a certain city there was a judge who neither feared God nor respected man. And there was a widow in that city who kept coming to him and saying, 'Give me justice against my adversary.' For a while he refused, but afterward he said to himself, 'Though I neither fear God nor respect man, yet because this widow keeps bothering me, I will give her justice, so that she will not beat me down by her continual coming.'" And the Lord said, "Hear what the unrighteous judge says. And will not God give justice to his elect, who cry to him day and night? Will he delay long over them? I tell you, he will give justice to them speedily. Nevertheless, when the Son of Man comes, will he find faith on earth?" (Luke 18:1-8 ESV)

Key Points: Luke 17:37 & 18:1-8

1. Prayer is to be like breathing. The only time we're conscious about it is when it's difficult to do it.
2. Your current breathing in prayer will keep you in good air, even though you're living in an environment where vultures (*stinking, rotten, decaying*) are circling (17:37).
3. Your current situation may be *stinking, rotten, and decaying*. Yet, Luke 18:1 tells us we should always pray. No matter your situation, pray! When we pray, it puts us in a different air/environment so we can ***breathe.***
4. The widow knew what the law said.
5. The widow asked for *"legal help" ("Get **legal help/ justice** for me from my adversary.")*.
6. The widow knew she had *"legal rights."*
7. The widow wasn't focused on the fact that the judge was unrighteous and didn't regard, respect, or revere God or care about her welfare. She knew what the ***law*** said.

The widow's persistence and aggressive approach toward the unjust judge were wearing him out.

> *"Yet because this woman troubles me, I will avenge her, lest, by her continual coming, she weary me." (Luke 18:5 NKJV)*

The Greek word for *"weary me"* means *"to give a black eye."* If the judge did not give her legal help, the widow would give the judge *a black eye* ***(ruin his reputation)***. And if she ruined his reputation, his status as a judge would be in the wind. After all this, in the widow's quest of getting her petition honored, the unrighteous judge had an awakening.

> *"And shall God not avenge His* ***own elect (that's you and me)*** *who cry out day and night to Him, though He bears long with them?" (Luke 18:7 NKJV)*

In other words, "*Who am I (the judge) not to grant her what she's petitioning?"* Look at what happened next:

> *"I tell you that He will avenge them '****speedily****' (quickly, expeditiously, suddenly, swiftly, rapidly, promptly, hurriedly)." (Luke 18:8a NKJV)*

She was granted justice from the unjust judge ***quickly***!

I have read this scripture a dozen or more times. Yet when Dr. Tony Evans dissected the scripture, it came to life. At the beginning of Pastor Evan's teaching, I was trying to connect the dots. But as I listened and focused, the Holy Spirit began to work with me to bring understanding and revelation.

> *"But the Helper, the Holy Spirit, whom the Father will send in my name, he will teach you all things and bring to your remembrance all that I have said to you."* (John 14:26-NKJV)

This scripture has given me enormous strength, substance, and sustainability to continue fighting for my healing during dialysis. It has allowed me to see God in a different light from a much different perspective of which I'd never experienced before. As I continued to listen and follow along with Dr. Evans' teaching, he took me to 1 John 5:14 (NKJV),

> *"Now this is the* ***confidence*** *that we have in Him, that if we* ***ask anything according to His will,*** *He hears us. And if we know that He hears us, whatever we ask, we know that we have the petitions that we have asked of Him."*

Wow! After reading this scripture and hearing Pastor Evans expound on the key points, I had to ask myself, *"How can I be certain I'm praying according to the will of God?"* My highest goal is to bring glory to God, and this includes praying according to His divine will. There are seven biblical principles to help Christians pray the will of God (this is by no means an exhaustive list, but it indicates what we are to pray for).

We should pray for things of which the Bible commands prayer. We are instructed to pray for our enemies.

- *"But I say to you, love your enemies, bless those who curse you, do good to those who hate you, and pray for those who spitefully use you and persecute you."* (Matthew 5:44 NKJV)

We should pray for God to send missionaries.

- *"Then He said to them, 'The harvest truly is great, but the laborers are few; therefore pray the Lord of the harvest to send out laborers into His harvest.'"* (Luke 10:2 NKJV)

We should pray that we do not enter into temptation.

- *"Watch and pray, lest you enter into temptation. The spirit indeed is willing, but the flesh is weak."* (Matthew 26:41 NKJV)

We should pray for ministers of the Word of God.

- *"Meanwhile praying also for us, that God would open to us a door for the word, to speak the mystery of Christ, for which I am also in chains."* (Colossians 4:3 NLT)

We should pray for government authorities.

- *"Therefore I exhort first of all that supplications, prayers, intercessions, and giving of thanks be made for all men, for kings and all who are in authority, that we may lead a quiet and peaceable life in all godliness and [c]reverence. For this is good and acceptable in the sight of God our Savior, who desires all men to be saved and to come to the knowledge of the truth."* (1 Timothy 2:1-4)

We should pray for relief from affliction.

- *"Is anyone among you suffering? Let him pray. Is anyone cheerful? Let him sing psalms. Is anyone among you sick? Let him call for the elders of the church, and let them pray over him, anointing him with oil in the name of the Lord. And the prayer of faith will save the sick, and the Lord will raise him up. And if he has committed sins, he will be forgiven."* (James 5:13-15 NKJV)

We should pray for the healing and wholeness of all Christians.

"Confess your trespasses to one another, and pray for one another, that you may be healed.

The effective fervent prayer of a righteous man avails much." (James 5:16 NKJV)

At this point, I was completely focused on 1 John 5:14. As he continued to dissect this passage of Scripture, I realized I needed to open my mouth and have a one-on-one conversation with God. It went something like this:

"Father, I need You to hear my heart, my soul, and this prayer. You're already well aware of my situation. However, I'm going to explain it again in case You may have forgotten. Your child has been on dialysis for eight years and five months. I'm not complaining, I'm not grumbling, I'm not bitter, and I'm not angry. However, my body and spirit are tired. There are days I don't feel well, but I seem to push through. There are days I don't want to go to treatment, yet I get up, get dressed, and press my way. I know You're there with me, and I also know that it's been You who has carried me through every treatment. I just read in Your Word where ***You said****, 'Because of my confidence, I can come to You and ask of* ***anything that's within Your will*** *and You will hear me'(1 John 5:14). Because I know You've heard me, whatever I ask, I can have what I've asked for.' That's what You said!*

Remember, this is what You've already ***decreed and declared****. I'm not making this up as I go. Father, this is what* ***You told me.*** *God, I'm asking You to respond to what* ***You said****. I'm having a conversation with You according to Your Word.*

I believe it's Your will that my kidney function is healed and restored. I believe it's Your will that I'm healthy, whole, and free of all impurities. And I also believe You want me available to You to be used to advance Your kingdom in the earth. Because You're sovereign and You can do whatever You want to do, it doesn't matter how You choose to restore my kidney function. That's Your call and Your will. Father, I ask that Your will be done, not mine! I'm calling on You to respond, react, and reveal Your power and glory to Your child. Remember, You also ***said*** *in Mark 11:24,* ***'Whatever I ask in prayer; believe that I have received it, it will be mine.'*** *I believe that my request has been signed, delivered, and sealed with Your blood. I receive. God, I ask all this in the mighty, matchless, and magnificent name of my Lord and Savior, Jesus Christ, Amen!"*

Praying in the Spirit:

- The best way to pray is to call on God to respond to His Word; call on Him to respond to His own truth.
- When all hell breaks loose, you have a unique ability to be aggressively ***specific.***
- When you bring *spiritual truth/God's Word* into your conversation with the Father, you are now praying in the Spirit.
- When we know exactly what God has already said and pray in respect of what He has said, it gives precedence, priority, and preeminence in the spiritual realm.

- The purpose of prayer is so that heaven can *occupy, overrun, and overrule* the earth—to bring heaven to earth, to bring the spiritual into the physical (*"On earth as it is in Heaven"* Matthew 6:10).

Upon completing my morning meditation and prayer, I sat quietly and reflected on what had just transpired. I had had an encounter with God! And I had never prayed with that much intensity and fervor.

'DAY TWO'

It was Sunday morning, December 15, 2019. As I was sitting in worship service, my cell phone rang. Of course, I had the phone on mute setting *(I didn't want it ringing during service)*. Around 10:45 am, I had an incoming call. I didn't recognize the number, nor did I recognize the name. So, I ignored it and returned to Pastor Reggie's sermon (I believe he was teaching from Numbers 13). He spoke these words as the first call was coming through. And this is what he said:

"In every promise, there's built-in trust—the ability to trust and rely on God."

He also spoke these words,

"Seeing yourself wrong and unworthy will always cause the promise of God to be delayed in your life."

Both of these principles hit home. At some stage of having dialysis, I had forgotten about the promises of God and relying on Him and in Him to get me through this challenge. It was time I step up and take God seriously. About an hour later, the same name and number appeared on my phone. This time, she decided to leave a voice message. After service, I had forgotten about the call until something within me said, *"Check your messages."* I checked my messages, and this is what I heard (I saved the message),

"Hi, this is Becky with the University of Chicago, trying to reach Mr. Lavender about a kidney offer. Can you please call me as soon as you get this message? My number here is ###-####-####. Thank you!"

I was knocked completely off my block! I sat in the car, weeping tears of amazement while trying to grasp what had just happened. The only thing I can attribute to what happened is the prayer I'd prayed on the previous day. Luke 18:8 says,

- *"I tell you that He will avenge them* ***speedily****." (NKJV)*
- *"I tell you, he will grant justice to them* ***quickly!****" (NLT)*
- *"I assure you, he will. He will not* ***drag his feet.****" (MSG)*

The first thing we must understand about God's timing is that it's always perfect. It's never out of sync. It's never out of rhythm. It's never out of order. It's never too late or too early. It's never a mistake, and it's never confused. Just as all His ways are perfect, all His ways are precise.

"As for God, His way is perfect; the Word of the Lord is flawless." (Psalm 18:30 NIV)

Throughout the day, I was in constant conversation with the transplant team at the University of Chicago. There were so many things I had to do before surgery. I was excited but at the same time very anxious. However, there was a protocol and procedure. A lot goes into transplantation surgery with regards to the patient and transplant team. God had brought me this far, and He would not leave me. As I was preparing to be admitted, I reflected on what Pastor Reggie had stated earlier,

"In every promise, there's built-in trust; the ability to trust and rely on God."

One of the promises of God is found in Deuteronomy 31:6,

"Be strong and of good courage, ***do not fear nor be afraid*** *of them; for the Lord your God, He is the One who goes with you.* ***He will not leave you nor forsake you."***

'DAY THREE'

It was Monday morning, December 16, 2019, and I was preparing to have my final dialysis treatment. I was reminded by the Holy Spirit, *"You had your first treatment on June 16, 2011, and now you're having your final treatment, December 16, 2019."* This meant I'd been dialyzing for eight years. To be exact, eight years and five months, a total of *1,212 treatments, of which I never missed a treatment.* I believe there's something spiritual about this transplant.

Full Disclaimer: First of all, I must emphasize that I'm in no way trying to promote any sort of psychic or mystical jargon as to get you to think I'm deep. I'm not! I'm also not trying to suggest that numbers will ever take the place of God's infallible Word. They will not! I'm only trying to make an observation from a spiritual perspective and something I've noticed in the Bible. For example, Jesus was resurrected in *three* days *(the biblical meaning of the number three: completeness, wholeness, and perfection).* Jesus had *twelve* disciples *(the biblical meaning of the number twelve: power and authority)*, and God is *three* in one *(the Holy Trinity: Father, Son, and Holy Spirit.)* Please allow me to explain.

While I was in the hospital preparing for surgery, I began thinking about what had happened over the weekend and the magnitude of the power of God. The numbers I will share with you aligned themselves biblically and prophetically.

- I dialyzed for eight years *(the biblical meaning of eight is "new beginnings")* and five months *(the biblical meaning of five is "grace").*
- I did 1,212 treatments *(the biblical meaning of the number twelve is "power and authority").*
- I prayed 1 John 5:14 *(chapter five/"grace", 1+4=5-"grace")*
- I prayed and had a lengthy conversation with God Saturday and had surgery Wednesday *(fifth day-"grace")*
- I had my first treatment June 16, ***2011,*** and my final treatment December 16, **2019** *(eight-year difference-"new beginnings"),* and June 16 and December 16, 1+6=7 *(the biblical meaning of the number seven is "completion and perfection").*
- I studied Luke 18:1-8, the widow and the unrighteous judge *(the number eight appears once again, "new beginnings").*

The number 8

- The number eight is used seventy-three times in the Bible.
- The number eight is the symbol of "*resurrection and regeneration.*"

- In the Bible, the number eight means *"new beginning;"* it denotes *a new order or creation.*
- In the Jewish culture, boys were to be *"circumcised on the eighth day"* (Leviticus 12:3 NIV).

The number 5

- The number five represents God's *grace, goodness, and favor* toward all humanity and is mentioned 318 times in Scripture.
- Five is the number of grace and multiplied by itself equals twenty-five—*grace upon grace.*
- The Ten Commandments contain two sets of five commandments. The first five commandments are related to our *"relationship with God."* The latter five commandments relate to our *"relationship with each other."*

The number 12

- The number *twelve* can be found in 187 places in the Bible. Revelation alone has twenty-two occurrences of the number.
- The number *twelve* symbolizes *God's "power and authority"*, as well as serving as a perfect governmental foundation.
- Jacob had *twelve* sons; each son represented one of the *twelve* tribes (Gen. 35:23-26).

- Ishmael was born to Abraham through Hagar, who also had *twelve* sons (Gen. 17:20).
- Jesus chose, called and commissioned *twelve* men to train, teach, and tutor and to bear witness to what He did and spread the gospel to the entire world (Matt. 10:1-4, Mark 3:13-19, Luke 6:12-16).

The number 7

- The number *seven* is one of the most significant numbers in the Bible. It symbolizes *completeness or perfection.*
- Shortly after God created the world, He rested on the *seventh* day (Gen. 2:2).
- Jacob's *seven* years of service to Laban (Gen. 29:18-30).
- Pharaoh's *seven* fat cows and *seven* lean cows (Gen. 41:27).
- The *seven* churches (Rev. 2-3).
- The *seven* trumpets and the *seven* priests who sounded them (Josh. 6:4).

As you can see, this is no coincidence. Nothing just happens! I believe these numbers are somehow linked to my eight years, five months of dialysis leading up to the transplant. After the Holy Spirit revealed this to me, I was determined to do more study regarding the meaning behind these numbers and how they're related to my situation.

I made it home from dialysis with a serious appetite (which meant I had a good treatment). While in the midst of preparing the meal, my transplant coordinator called and informed me that the surgeons would like for me to be admitted into the hospital by 5:30 pm so they could begin preparing me for surgery. Don't forget, I had packed a year earlier (first offer, March 1, 2018). It was just a matter of my grabbing my overnight bag and heading out the door. I was only eight minutes from the hospital. When I arrived at the hospital, the transplant team met with me to explain the dilemma of them not having the organ. It was a matter of waiting for the donor organ to be removed and released to the hospital. They were not able to do the surgery on Monday as scheduled. So, we waited.

'DAY FOUR'

It was Tuesday, December 17, 2019, and the morning was starting to be one of excitement, energy, and enthusiasm. By this time, the doctors were still under the impression the organ would be accessible so they could proceed with surgery. It was still not available. However, the transplant team did share with me information regarding my donor. The donor was a forty-two-year-old male who was "brain dead." They continued sharing with me the condition, longevity, and status of the kidney. What they shared with me was both good and not-so-good news. After all, I was getting a kidney from a deceased individual. There is a risk when you're the recipient of a kidney from a person who has died.

Deceased-donor kidneys come from people who have died suddenly, usually from an accident or bleed into the brain. These individuals are usually between one and seventy years of age and have been relatively healthy before their death (Jefferson University Hospital).

To be truthfully honest, I had no worries. Of course, there were some concerns. I was quite content with the entire process, though, and I was at peace because I knew this was all God's doing. The nurses and transplant team kept me informed regarding the time of the surgery and what I needed to do to prepare myself. There's so much that goes into the genesis stage of the procedure. For me, the most challenging element before surgery was my emotions. They were bouncing off the hospital walls. What helped me stay focused and kept my emotions in check was walking the hospital halls every three to four hours. The doctors recommended that I do this quite often.

Later that evening, the surgeon came and informed me that the organ was ready to be transported and that the surgery was scheduled for Wednesday.

'DAY FIVE'

It was day *five*, Wednesday morning, December 18, 2019. I was wide awake with excitement, preparing to dive into my morning meditation. I had left my Bible at home, so I was using my cell phone and tablet. It's rather difficult to study in the hospital when the nurses, students, housekeeping, and doctors are invading your space. I wished there was some way I could lock the doors for thirty minutes so I could at least get some quiet time with God. This simply would not happen this morning. I figured I might as well get up and do some walking to keep my anxiety level down.

This was the day of the surgery, and the doctors had not disclosed a time for the procedure. What I was hearing from the nurses is that the surgeons had to wait until the OR (operating room) give them a time to perform the surgery. It was important that they give me a time so I could notify my family and friends. I didn't want them to inform me at the last minute. That would not allow them enough traveling time, seeing that some were coming quite a distance. While I was waiting, the nurse came in to inform me of the time I would be transported to be prepped for surgery. This was exciting and terrifying! It was terrifying because I'd never had a transplant. The idea of having another person's organ implanted into my body was mind-boggling. This brings me to this point. God knew what He was doing when He designed the human body. It's amazing how God has given surgeons the skill and knowledge to take an organ from a *deceased* person and implant the organ into another person to keep him or her alive. Only God can do this and no one else! While I was being transported to surgery, I asked God this question, *"Is there anything You cannot do*?" The only thing God cannot do is act contrary to His character, nature, and Word. Let's take a look at a few scriptures:

- **He cannot lie:** *"In hope of eternal life which God, who cannot lie, promised before time began."* (Titus 1:2 NKJV)
- **He cannot sin, because He's holy:** *"Because it is written, 'Be holy, for I am holy.'"* (1 Peter 1:16 NKJV)
- **He cannot and will not overlook sin because He's just. Jesus paid the price and penalty for our sin:** *"To demonstrate at present His righteousness, that He might be just and the justifier of the one who has faith in Jesus."* (Romans 3:26 NKJV)
- **He cannot *ignore* His Word; He must *respond* to His own Word:** *"So shall My word be that goes forth from My mouth; It shall not return to Me void, But it shall accomplish what I please, And it shall prosper in the thing for which I sent it."* (Isaiah 55:11 NKJV)

As the time approached for me to be transported for surgery, my nerves and anxiety were through the roof. I didn't know what to think. I couldn't believe I was having a kidney transplant. This was mind-blowing. Only God could orchestrate such a powerful move as this. Proverbs 16:9 (MSG) says,

> *"We plan the way we want to live, but only God makes us able to live it."*

What's the meaning of the word *"orchestra or orchestrates"*?

When I think of the word orchestrates, I immediately think of music. I, being a musician, of course my mind would take me into the realm of music.

- To orchestrate is to arrange or score (music) for orchestral performance
- An orchestra is a group of instrumentalists, especially one combining string, woodwind, brass, and percussion sections and playing classical music

Look at the similarities. God plans, arranges, organizes, adapts, scores, sets up, and puts together a plan for our lives that plays in *harmony* with His plan and His will. God would use the amputations, dialysis, and transplant to *orchestrate, organize, arrange, adapt, plan, set up*, and put together my life to impact the lives of others and bring Him glory. He wanted me to understand that it was His power working to orchestrate and organize my life so that others could see His power through my challenges.

My sisters arrived at the hospital to be with me during the transplant. It was around 2:00 pm, and I was hurled off to be prepped for surgery. This process would take some time. Once I arrived at the holding area, my emotions, anxiety, and nerves were under control. The transplant team met me and my family, and they thoroughly explained the procedure to make certain the family understood what was about to take place and answer any questions or concerns they might have. The nurse gave me what she called a *"mild sedative."* Before I knew anything, I was sleeping like a baby. The surgery took four hours, recovery one hour, and then back in my room around 10:30 pm that evening. Once again,

> *"This is the Lords' doing; it is marvelous in our eyes."* (Psalm 118:23 KJV)

CHAPTER FIVE

CRISIS: A REASON TO PRAY

> *"Then you will call upon Me and go and pray to Me, and I will listen to you."* (Jeremiah 29:12 NKJV)

What is prayer?

"Earthly permission for heavenly interference; Earth giving heaven permission to interfere or to intervene in what's happening in my world of reality from the spiritual point of view; relational communication with God" (Dr. Tony Evans).

What is a crisis?

"A time when a difficult or important decision must be made"

I have desperately tried to bring to the forefront my battle, frustration, fight, trials, and triumphs of being on dialysis for eight years. In addition to sharing about being on dialysis, I have shared with you the "power of God" through prayer when God *expeditiously* granted my request to restore my kidney function. I have discovered that when we have a crisis, it should drive us closer to the Lord and not away from Him.

In John 11, Mary and Martha went to Jesus with a serious crisis. Their brother Lazarus was sick. Jesus had a close relationship with the family. When Lazarus was sick, it was natural for them to bring their need to Jesus. It was expected that if He miraculously met the needs of so many others, He would meet their need.

> *"Therefore the sisters sent to Him saying, 'Lord, behold he whom You love is sick.'"* (John 11:3)

> *"Jesus loved Martha and her sister and Lazarus."* (John 11:5)

> *"The love of Jesus does not separate us from the common necessities and infirmities*

of human life. Men of God are still men."
(Charles Spurgeon)

Newsflash: Believers get sick!

As I studied this scripture, I noticed that Mary and Martha did not specifically ask Jesus to heal their brother. They felt as if there was no need. However, they did take Lazarus to Him and tell Him what the crisis was. *They went to Jesus for help in their time of crisis.* This narrative shows believers that especially during times of crisis, they should go to God with their petition. *These scriptures also teach us that one can be a believer and enjoy intimacy with God yet be right in the middle of a crisis.* What's important is that we don't view our crisis as a gauge of our spirituality or as a reason to distance ourselves from intimacy with the Father. Instead, we must trust that even in our times of trouble, God will reveal His greater glory as He promptly works things out for our good. Let's take a look at John 9:1-3 (NIV):

> *"As he went along, he saw a man blind from birth. His disciples asked him, 'Rabbi, who sinned, this man or his parents, that he was born blind?' 'Neither this man nor his parents sinned,' said Jesus, 'but this happened so that the works of God might be displayed in him.'"*

Please, please focus on the latter part of this scripture, *"But this happened so that the works of God might be displayed in him."* Displayed in who? ***The blind man***!

Jesus wanted His disciples to know it would be God Himself to heal the blind man of his crisis and no one else. God wants all the credit, glory, recognition, accolades, and grandeur. All the glory is centered around one person. He is the only audience, *an audience of one*! He tells us in Isaiah 42:8 (NLT),

> *"**I** (God) am the Lord; that is **My** name! **I will not** give **My** glory to anyone else, nor share **My** praise with carved idols."*

Nothing happens in our lives without our Father's permission, and He will not allow a difficulty unless He has a divine purpose for it. In most cases, God will allow things to happen, or He can keep and block things from happening. In either case, the crises, challenges, issues, or difficulties are designed to build *character, conduct, integrity, and our intimacy with God*. He wants to show Himself as God! This is what Jeremiah said in Lamentations 3:37-38 (NLT),

> *"Who can command things to happen without the Lord's permission? Does not the Most High send both **calamity and good**?"*

When I was going through my crisis *(both amputations)*, I had concluded that God was a million miles away from me *(so I thought)*. I would pray and pray for Him to hear me and answer my prayers. This went on for weeks, months, and even some years. Yet, I never gave up hope that He would at some point respond to my petition. I was studying with Dr. Evans' teaching from this subject, "*Praying and Waiting for God's Timing*." During this session, he gives key points regarding prayer.

- There must be a point of contact *(prayer)* between you and God to experience His power and supernatural provision.
- Without a point of contact *(prayer)*, you don't experience what the provision is.
- The point of contact between your need and God's provision is *prayer*.
- *Prayer* is the mechanism God has decreed that is necessary for Him to *"release"* what He intends.
- *Prayer* does not make God do what He had not planned to do. But what it does is *"release"* God to do what He decreed to do.
- Where there is no *prayer*, there is no contact, and where there is no contact, you do not get what God has already decreed and declared for you to have as His will.
- *Prayer* is the one thing God has established to make contact with what He has already decreed.

- *Prayer* activates the decree and the will of God.

The result I was so desperately seeking and longing for was in my prayer life and language. If I was to experience what God wanted to release into my life, I had to make the right connection and the point of contact *(prayer)* top priority. Because my prayer life was deficient, dull, and dry, it became very challenging when it seemed as if God didn't care about my situation and when I thought He wasn't there when I was in trouble. The Word of God decreed something completely different from my way of thinking, and this is what He had already declared,

> *"God is our refuge and strength, a very present help in trouble."* (Psalm 46:1 NKJV)

In John 11:21, Martha expressed her disappointment that Jesus wasn't around when her brother died. Both she and her sister wondered why Jesus had not only been absent on the day that Lazarus died but had delayed His arrival by two days. It's okay to have a legitimate concern, to question Him, and to be honest with God in a crisis. When we're transparent, upfront, and honest with God, He is not surprised. While our emotions are real, raw, and rigid, we shouldn't lean on our emotions and understanding *("Lean not on your own understanding"—Prov. 3:5)* because they have the greatest potential to steer us in a direction that our flesh will regret later in life. Our emotions should always drive us toward God, and not away from God. He is the Author and Finisher of our faith.

How could I focus on praying when I didn't think God was listening? There were times I did not feel like praying because I had no more strength to talk to Him. I was in a dry, desolate, and desperate place, and my thoughts of positioning myself to have a conversation with God weren't there. "*How do I lift my darkest, most depressed, most lonely moments to God? How can I pray when I'm most deeply alone, helpless, and my whole world seems to be crashing and crumbling all around me*?" There had to be a solution to my crisis.

I had to get out of my comfort zone; this state of depression, and delve into the Word of God for comfort and strength. Just as I was preparing to compose this manuscript, I was listening to Dr. Tony Evans, and he made this profound statement,

> "*God will allow things in our lives that may not be preferential but will bring Him glory.*"

What a revelation! *A light came on. Now I was able to see the panoramic view, the entire picture.*

What I preferred was not in the will of God, and what I preferred would not bring Him what He deserves, glory! Yes, I was depressed, but God would use my depression to shed light on who He is. This had very little to do with me and my emotions and tantrums. After hearing this powerful statement, I posed this question to the Father: *"God, what glory do You want from my crisis?"*

He replied, *"My **living** Word must always lead you back to My **written** Word."* According to Hebrews 4:12-ESV,

> *"For the word of God is living and active, sharper than any two-edged sword, piercing to the division of soul and of spirit, of joints and of marrow, and discerning the thoughts and intentions of the heart."*

According to Hebrews 4:12, the Bible has potent power in and of itself. The written Word of God accomplishes God's purposes.

Which meant, I needed God's power (*living Word*) to accomplish His purpose (*written Word*). It was time that I opened my mouth and cry out to Him in prayer. It was time I set aside everything that would try and hinder my relationship with God. It was time I put prayer in its proper place, posture, perspective, practice, and position! Prayer was the key to God releasing what He had already decreed.

What is the *goal* of prayer?

- The goal of prayer is to make heaven visible on earth.
- The goal of prayer is to get God to release heaven on earth.

- The goal of prayer is to get eternity to make a statement in time.
- The goal of prayer is to "*draw*" from heaven into *earth*.

What is the *power* of prayer?

- The power of prayer is the power of God, who hears and answers prayer. (Luke 1:37)
- The power of prayer should be like breathing. The only time when you're conscious about breathing is when it's difficult to do it. (Dr. Tony Evans)
- Prayer to God should be persistent and consistent. (Luke 18:1-8)
- God invites us to pray to Him. (Jeremiah 33:3)
- God hears the prayers of His children. He commands us to petition His throne, and He promises to listen when we do. (Psalm 18:6)

The power of prayer does not flow from us; it doesn't have selective words or special vernacular we use or the special way we speak it or even how often we speak it. The power of prayer is not based on a certain path we've traveled, a particular challenge we've faced, or a certain position of our bodies. The power of prayer does not come from the use of idols, icons, candles, crafts, beads, or bangles. ***The power of prayer comes from the Omnipotent One, the Holy One of Israel, who hears our prayers and answers them.***

Prayer places us in direct contact *(point of contact)* with the Father, and we should expect extraordinary, miraculous, and astounding results, whether or not He chooses to grant our petitions or deny our requests. Whatever answer He chooses to give us regarding our prayers, the God to whom we pray is the source of the power of prayer, and He can and will answer us according to His perfect will and timing, ***not ours.*** Matthew 6:10 (KJV) says,

> *"Thy Kingdom come, Thy will be done, in earth as it is in Heaven."*

> *"Our prayers should reach heaven and pull the spiritual realm down to earth to manifest itself in the physical realm!"*

I accepted the Lord Jesus Christ at the age of seven. The entire duration of my fifty-year journey, I've concluded that prayer can be a daunting *mystery*, not in the sense that it's spooky, scary, or even sinister. When I speak of prayer being a daunting mystery, I'm referring to prayer as being *"difficult to comprehend and understand."* In so many ways, prayer is one of the most misinterpreted and misunderstood tools of a believer's life. There were so many times I wondered if God was listening to my prayer. Did my prayer have any effect on my life? What is an acceptable prayer, and what's not acceptable? How am I to pray to the Father? Is there a prayer I can use as a model? Let's take a look at several reasons why we should pray and its benefits.

- We pray because it's a privilege. God is sovereign, sacred and set apart, completely holy and only accessible insomuch as He reveals Himself to us. Prayer is His way of inviting us to get to know Him. Because of His infinite qualities, character, nature, and being, He allows us to come near Him. He wants it and desires it. Prayer is our "*relational communication with God*." Just as friends and family members spend time talking and communicating with one another to deepen and strengthen their relationships, so prayer deepens and strengthens our relationship with our Father (Phil. 4:6, James 5:16, Jer. 29:12, Jer. 33:3, Luke 6:27-28).

Jesus set an excellent example and model of ***prayer*** for us. The gospels indicate several times that Jesus ***prayed***. John 17 is possibly one of the greatest portraits. If Jesus, who is God, ***prayed*** to the Father, how much more should we? (John 17, Heb. 5:7, Luke 3:21, Matt. 14:23, Mark 6:26).

- ***Prayer*** draws us closer to God, which leads us into the very presence of the Father. It also allows us to worship and adore Him, which has a major impact on our lives. James 1:5 (NKJV) says,

*"If any of you lacks wisdom, **let him ask God,** who gives liberally and without reproach, and it will be given to him."*

- ***Prayer*** can lead us to wisdom. Colossians 1:9 (NKJV) says,

*"For this reason, we also, since the day we heard it, do not cease to pray for you, and to ask that you may be filled with the knowledge of His will in all **wisdom** and spiritual understanding."*

- ***Prayer*** can relieve our anxiety. Philippians 4:6-9 (MSG) says,

*"Don't fret or worry. Instead of worrying, **pray.** Let petitions and praises shape your worries into **prayers,** letting God know your concerns. Before you know it, a sense of God's wholeness, everything coming together for good, will come and settle you down. It's wonderful what happens when Christ displaces worry at the center of your life. Summing it all up, friends, I'd say you'll do best by filling your minds and meditating on things true, noble, reputable, authentic, compelling, gracious—the best, not the worst; the beautiful, not*

> *the ugly; things to praise, not things to curse. Put into practice what you learned from me, what you heard and saw and realized. Do that, and God, who makes everything work together, will work you into his most excellent harmonies."*

When we approach God with the desires of our hearts and our desires align themselves with His desires, fulfil His will, and expand His kingdom on the earth, He hears us and responds to our desires. Prayer is an intimate interaction with God. It brings Him glory, and it gives us insight and revelation into who He is and has a palpable effect on our lives. Prayer is a privilege and a spiritual discipline that impacts every area of our lives.

What is the proper way to pray?

Is it best to pray standing up, sitting down, kneeling, or bowing down? Should our hands be open, closed, or lifted toward God? Do our eyes need to be open or closed when we pray? Is it better to pray in a church building, our homes, on the job, in the car, in the store, or out in nature? Should we pray in the morning when we get up or at night before we go to bed? Are there certain words we need to say in our prayers? How do we begin our prayers? What is the proper way to close a prayer? These questions, and others are common questions asked about prayer. What is the proper way to pray? Do any of the above things even matter?

Far too often, prayer is viewed as a *"magic formula."* Some believe that if we do not say exactly the right things or pray in the right position, God will not hear and answer our prayer. *This is not true*! God does not answer our prayers based on when we pray, where we pray, what position our body is in, or in what order we word our prayers. We are told in 1 John 5:14-15,

> *"To have* ***confidence*** *(trust, faith, belief) when we come to God in prayer, knowing He hears us and will grant* ***whatever we ask as long as it is in His will."***

Similarly, John 14:13 (NKJV) declares,

> *"And whatever you ask in My name, that I will do, that the Father may be glorified in the Son.*
>
> ***"If you ask anything in My name, I will do it."***

According to these and many other scriptures, God answers prayer requests based on whether they are asked according to His will.

So, what is the proper way to pray? Philippians 4:6-7 tells us,

> *"Do not be anxious about anything, but in everything by prayer and petition, with thanksgiving, present your request to God".*

The proper way to pray is to pour out our hearts to God, being honest, transparent and open with Him as He already knows us better than we know ourselves. We are to present our requests to God, keeping in mind that God knows what is best and will not grant a request that is not His will for us. We are to express our love, gratitude, and worship to God in prayer without worrying about having just the right words to say. ***God is more interested in the content of our hearts than the eloquence of our words.***

The closest the Bible comes to giving a "*pattern*" for prayer is the Lord's Prayer in Matthew 6:9-13. Please understand that the Lord's Prayer is not a prayer we are to memorize and recite to God. It is a model of the things that should go into a prayer—*worship, trust in God, requests, confession, and submission* (Got questions.org).

Going through the *trauma* of the amputations and the *triumph* of receiving the kidney transplant positioned me to be in a place of peace. The Holy Spirit was teaching me to embrace the pain and allow it to draw me closer to the Father. Because God is sovereign, He will either allow the pain, or He will block the pain. In either case, the pain is working for my good and His glory.

> *"Pain is always an indication to pray, and God will always allow pain, crisis, and frustration to linger because He's trying to get us to pray."*

We all experience pain in life, whether emotional or physical pain. No pain is alike; we must all walk the journey and path that God has for us. Yet, God promises that there is a purpose in all pain. God will never waste pain. God will never waste a tear, and He will never waste an opportunity to be God! We can press on each day knowing that our God loves us and wants to use the hurt and pain in this world to bring Him glory. I have equipped you with several Bible verses to help you understand the purpose of pain in your life and encourage you to find joy in the middle and midst of your pain. Please don't give up hope. God has so much more for your life, even in dialysis.

SEVEN WAYS YOUR PAIN HAS A PURPOSE

1. Pain allows you to discover your own strength.
2. Pain matures you.
3. Pain leverages the suffering in your life for God's greater glory and your purpose.

4. Pain reflects things in you that you need to see, address and ask God for help so that you can move toward your purpose.
5. Pain prepares you for your created purpose and calling.
6. Pain deepens your faith, endurance, perseverance, character, and strength.
7. Pain forces you to pay attention to the work the Holy Spirit is doing inside of you.

THE END

Closing Remarks

"Fulfill my joy by being like-minded, having the same love, being of one accord, of one mind. Let nothing be done through selfish ambition or conceit, but in lowliness of mind let each esteem others better than himself. Let each of you look out not only for his own interests but also for the interests of others." (Philippians 2:2-4 NKJV).

For quite some time, I've wanted to write my story regarding my experiences and challenges of being on dialysis. It's amazing how God presents us with opportunities that allow us to fulfill what we desire to do. Not knowing when I would be able to compose this book. One week after the surgery, the Holy Spirit compelled me to begin the process on New Year's Day 2020. When that's the time most of the country is celebrating a new era in history,

I was at the computer. Immediately after the transplant, I had a window of recovery, rest, reflection, and refreshment time. So, why not utilize the time to empower the lives of others? I'm so grateful I responded to what my spirit was prompting.

In my introduction, I mentioned how selfish and self-absorbed I had become because I didn't want to share my story. As I began writing, I had several memories of others helping me adjust to the dynamics and regimen dialysis required. I also begin to think of the many instances others came to my rescue when the treatments became overwhelming and frightening.

I believe it's my charge, duty, and responsibility to help those who are currently on dialysis and those who will be starting the process. Every circumstance we're faced with and every challenge that presents itself allows us to make a difference in the lives of others. There was a reason I was on dialysis for eight years. There was a reason God preserved my life through the difficulties of having to endure the many health issues attached to the discomfort of end-stage renal dis-ease.

In Philippians 2:4 (NKJV), it says,

> *"Let each of you look out not only for his* ***own interests*** *but also for the* ***interests of others.****"*

This scripture was speaking directly to me, and it spoke volumes! Yes, I did go through dialysis, but I could not idly sit back and not use what God had brought me through. It is my mission and mandate to help those who are dealing with this treatment. Look at 2 Corinthians 1:4 (NKJV):

> *"Who comforts us in all our tribulation, that we may be able to comfort those who are in any trouble, with the comfort with which we ourselves are comforted by God."*

Now that God has comforted me through the treatment, the charge is laid upon my *heart, hands, and head*. I must return the same "*comfort*" I received from God and pass it on to others. The fact that I've gone through eight years of dialysis can help so many others.

Often, God will provide opportunities for us to walk with those during their pain. My dialysis treatments show how God will use my pain for good, bringing Him glory. I pray this book will bring you *"beauty for ashes, the oil of gladness instead of mourning, and a garment of praise instead of a spirit of despair" (Isaiah 61:3a)*. Be encouraged and stay encouraged!

I pray this prayer will bring you comfort, consolation, and contentment on your journey of dialysis.

Dialysis Patient's Prayer

Heavenly Father, the giver of life and every good and perfect gift, You are the Great I AM—my sustainer, my source, my refuge, and my strength. You are the Highest God, strong and mighty and mighty in battle. Thank you for this day...a day called *today*. Thank you for this day, a day I've never seen before. I realize and recognize Your mercies are new every morning. Great is Your faithfulness.

Thank You, O, God for waking me up this morning and starting this day with new mercies and new grace. Lord, You are holy above all things, and all the strength that I will ever need is found in Your hands. Father, there are sins I know of and sins I'm not aware of. I ask that You forgive me for all my iniquities and anything that I've done to grieve Your heart.

O God, I come boldly before You for comfort and relief to Your servant ***(insert your name)***. Heavenly Father, I ask that You give me Your power of healing, Your power of resilience, Your power of energy, Your power of rest, and Your power of a sound mind. You said, "*By Your stripes, I am healed" (Isaiah 53:5b).* I am healed according to Your divine Word. You also said, "*Your grace is sufficient for me, for Your power is made perfect in* my *weakness" (2 Corinthians 12:9a).* I require Your strength in my weakness, and I have every confidence in Your loving care and comfort through Your Son, Jesus Christ our Lord.

Sometimes I feel like I can't go on. I admit, Lord, sometimes it is hard. The pain, the discomfort, the anxiety, and the fear are too much for me, and I know that I don't have the strength on my own to go through this. Remember, You said, "*You didn't give me the spirit of fear...but of love, of power and a sound mind" (2 Timothy 1:7).*

Jesus, I know I can come to You and You will hear my prayer. I know that it's not Your intent to bring me to this journey just to leave me by myself. You said, "*You will never leave me nor forsake me" (Deuteronomy 31:6b, Hebrews 13:5b).* I trust You to carry me through this season, and I believe You can and You will manifest Your presence in my life and this health challenge.

Please, Lord, give me the strength that I need to face today. You told me not to worry about tomorrow. Tomorrow has enough worries of its own. If I must go through dialysis, I ask that You go through with me—every step, every move, every motion, every twist, every turn, and every tear. Lord,

I'm not asking that You take this challenge away. But I am asking that Your will be done.

Keep me from sinning during this trial. Instead, help me to keep my eyes on You. You are the Holy Lord, the Holy One of Israel, and all of my hope rests in You.

Thank You for hearing my prayer and responding to my prayer. I pray this in the mighty, matchless, magnificent, marvelous, and majestic name of Jesus Christ.

Amen!

Bibliography

The Bible

- Holy Bible: *New King James Version.* Review and Herald
- Peterson, Eugene H. *The Message.* NavPress, 2004
- *New Living Translation.* Tyndale House Publishers, 1996
- *The Holy Bible*: New International Version, Zondervan. 1958
- Siewert, Frances E. *The Amplified Bible.* Zondervan. 1958
- The Holy Bible: *King James Version.* Thomas Bay Press, 2000
- *The Living Bible.* Tyndale House, 1992
- *English Standard Version* (ESV). Crossway Bibles, Good News Publishers, 2001

Citations

-New York Center for Plastic & Laser Surgery, "***Article, Hyperbaric Oxygen Therapy for Wound Healing***", **Dr. Jacona, http://newyorkfacialplasticsurgery.com, November 2019**

-Jefferson University Hospital, "*Article, Deceased Donor Kidney Transplant*", http://www. hospitals.jefferson.edu, Dr. Adam S. Bozdin, M.D., November 2019

-Dr. Tony Evans, Twitter Statement, "*Sermon-The Test of Faith*", http://www.wordofyeshua.eu, August 11, 2015, Oakcliff Bible Church

Dr. Tony Evans, "*Sermon-Prayer That Works*", http:// www.tonyevans.org, Youtube, May 13, 2019, Oakcliff Bible Church

-Spurgeon, Charles Haddon, Sermon of the Week, "*Beloved and Yet Afflicted*", August 19, 2019, http://www. spurgeon.org

-Got Questions/Your Questions, Biblical Answers, "*What Is the Proper Way to Pray*?" November 2019, http://www. gotquestions.org

Endnotes

1. Oxford Languages, s.v. Online "*orchestrate*" accessed, August 2, 2020 http:/www.Lexico.com

2. Oxford Languages, s.v. Online "*orchestra*" accessed, August 2, 2020 http:/www.Lexico.com

3. Oxford Languages, s.v. Online "*crisis*" accessesd, August 2, 2020 http:/www.Lexico.com

About the Author

Born in Monroe, Louisiana, and migrating to the city of Chicago, Illinois, Zachary began his musical journey at the tender age of ten. Zachary's training was helmed by some of Chicago's finest in the area of choral, church, and vocal music. He has done extensive training in voice pedagogy at Roosevelt University/Chicago Musical College under the guidance of Mr. Robert Long and Ms. Ruth Ann Bishop.

Throughout his forty-six-year tenure as a church musician, Zachary has built a reputation for developing singers and musicians for the perfecting of the church's music ministry. He is passionate about the needs and objectives of church music and the future generation of singers and musicians. He specializes in bringing the talent and gift of the musicians to the forefront and allowing them to minister at their fullest capacity.

Zachary has continued to hone his skills as a composer, conductor, teacher, musician, and author and counts it all joy, honor, and privilege to be chosen by God to help lead the church in music excellence and provide an avenue for those who desire to be whole and healed.

CPSIA information can be obtained
at www.ICGtesting.com
Printed in the USA
LVHW080311151220
674208LV00015B/776